Honey

Jilly

Willow

Above Ava, opposite Charity

This page Nancy,
opposite page Lissa

Nora

Beth

Erin

Above Ebony, opposite Josie

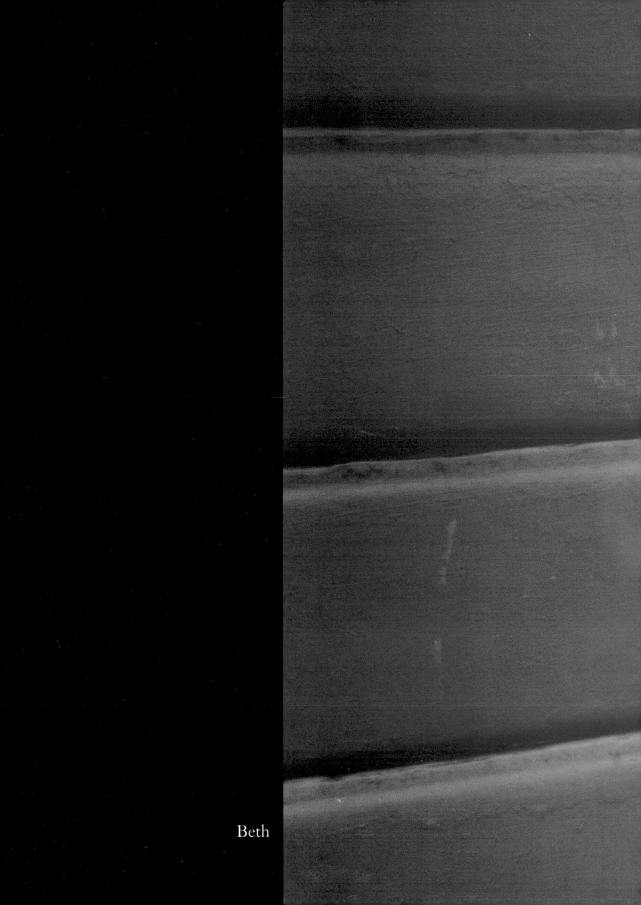

Beth

Casey

# RIBBON TWIST COLLECTION

## Index

Alpha

## No 1

# HONEY

## KIM HARGREAVES

### YARN

|  | XS | S | M | L | XL |  |
|---|---|---|---|---|---|---|
| To fit bust | 81 | 86 | 91 | 97 | 102 | cm |
|  | 32 | 34 | 36 | 38 | 40 | in |

**Rowan Ribbon Twist**

|  | 8 | 8 | 9 | 9 | 9 | x 100gm |

(photographed in Riches 116)

### NEEDLES

1 pair 10mm (no 000) (US 15) needles
1 pair 12mm (US 17) needles

### TENSION

8 sts and 11 rows to 10 cm measured over stocking stitch using 12mm (US 17) needles.

**Pattern note**: As row end edges form actual finished front opening edges of garment, it is important these edges are kept neat. Therefore avoid joining in new balls of yarn at these edges.

### HEM BORDER

Cast on 75 (75: 87: 87: 87) sts using 12mm (US 17) needles.
**Rows 1 and 2:** Purl.
**Row 3 (RS):** K2, *yfwd, K4, sl 2, K1, p2sso, K4, yfwd, K1, rep from * to last st, K1.
**Row 4 and every foll alt row:** K1, P to last st, K1.
**Row 5:** K2, *K1, yfwd, K3, sl 2, K1, p2sso, K3, yfwd, K2, rep from * to last st, K1.
**Row 7:** K2, *K2, yfwd, K2, sl 2, K1, p2sso, K2, yfwd, K3, rep from * to last st, K1.
**Row 9:** K2, *K3, yfwd, K1, sl 2, K1, p2sso, K1, yfwd, K4, rep from * to last st, K1.
**Row 11:** K2, *K4, yfwd, sl 2, K1, p2sso, yfwd, K5, rep from * to last st, K1.
**Row 13:** Knit.

**Row 15:** K17 (17: 20: 20: 20), K2tog, K1, K2tog tbl, K31 (31: 37: 37: 37), K2tog, K1, K2tog tbl, K to end. 71 (71: 83: 83: 83) sts.
**Row 17:** Knit.
**XS and S sizes**
**Row 19:** K3, (yfwd, K2tog, K4) twice, yfwd, K2tog, K3, (yfwd, K2tog, K4) twice, yfwd, K2tog, K3, K2tog tbl, yfwd, (K4, K2tog tbl, yfwd) twice, K3, K2tog tbl, yfwd, (K4, K2tog tbl, yfwd) twice, K3.
**M, L and XL sizes**
**Row 19:** K2, (yfwd, K2tog, K4) 6 times, yfwd, K2tog, K3, K2tog tbl, yfwd, (K4, K2tog tbl, yfwd) 6 times, K2.
**Divide for back and fronts**
**Row 20 (WS):** K1, P8 (18: 5: 9: 21), (P2tog) 1 (0: 1: 1: 0) times, (P6, P2tog) 0 (0: 1: 0: 0) times, P8 (0: 6: 10: 0) and slip these 18 (19: 20: 21: 22) sts onto a holder for left front, P9 (33: 6: 11: 39), (P2tog) 1 (0: 1: 1: 0) times, (P11, P2tog tbl, P9) 1 (0: 0: 0: 0) times, (P6, P2tog, P7, P2tog tbl, P6, P2tog tbl, P6) 0 (0: 1: 0: 0) times, (P13, P2tog tbl, P11) 0 (0: 0: 1: 0) times and slip these 31 (33: 35: 37: 39) sts onto another holder for back, P8 (0: 6: 10: 0), (P2tog tbl, P6) 0 (0: 1: 0: 0) times, (P2tog tbl) 1 (0: 1: 1: 0) times, P8 (18: 5: 9: 21), K1.
Cont on this last set of 18 (19: 20: 21: 22) sts only for right front.

### RIGHT FRONT

**Row 1 (RS):** Knit.
**Row 2:** P to last st, K1.
These 2 rows set the sts for the right front – front opening edge st in garter st with all other sts in st st.
Keeping sts correct as set, cont as folls:
Work 4 rows, ending with a WS row.
**Row 7 (inc) (RS):** K to last 2 sts, M1, K2. 19 (20: 21: 22: 23) sts.
Work 5 rows.

**Row 7:** Using yarn B, K2tog, (K1, yfwd, K1) all into next st, *sl 1, (K1, yfwd, K1) all into next st; rep from * to last 2 sts, K2tog. 23 sts.
**Row 8:** As row 2.
Break off yarn B and cont using yarn A only.
Beg with a K row, work in st st for 14 rows, dec 1 st at each end of 3rd of these rows and ending with a WS row. 21 sts.
**Row 23 (inc) (RS):** K2, M1, K to last 2 sts, M1, K2. 23 sts.
Working all increases as set by last row, inc 1 st at each end of every foll 10th (10th: 6th: 6th: 4th) row to 27 sts, then on every foll – (–: 8th: 8th: 6th) row until there are – (–: 29: 29: 31) sts.
Cont straight until sleeve measures 43 (43: 44: 44: 44) cm, ending with a WS row.

**Shape top**
Cast off 2 sts at beg of next 2 rows.
23 (23: 25: 25: 27) sts.
Dec 1 st at each end of next and foll alt row, then on foll 4th row, then on every foll alt row to 11 sts, then on foll row, ending with a WS row.
Cast off rem 9 sts.

## MAKING UP
**PRESS** as described on the information page.
Join both shoulder seams using back stitch, or mattress stitch if preferred.

**Collar**
With RS facing, using 12mm (US 17) needles and yarn A, slip 4 sts from right front holder onto right needle, rejoin yarn and pick up and knit 11 (11: 11: 13: 13) sts up right side of neck, 16 (16: 16: 18: 18) sts from back, and 11 (11: 11: 13: 13) sts down left side of neck, then K4 from left front holder.
46 (46: 46: 52: 52) sts.
**Row 1 (RS of collar, WS of body):** Knit.
**Row 2:** K4, P to last 4 sts, K4.
**Rows 3 and 4:** As rows 1 and 2.
**Row 5:** K16, (M1, K2, M1, K1) 4 (4: 4: 6: 6) times, M1, K2, M1, K16. 56 (56: 56: 66: 66) sts.
**Row 6:** As row 2.
Now rep rows 1 and 2 until collar measures 12 cm from pick-up row, inc 1 st at centre of last row and ending with RS of collar facing for next row.
57 (57: 57: 67: 67) sts.
Join in yarn B.

**Next row (RS):** Using yarn B, K1, (K1, yfwd, K1) all into next st, *sl 1, (K1, yfwd, K1) all into next st; rep from * to last st, K1.
**Next row:** Using yarn B, K1, K3tog tbl, *sl 1, K3tog tbl, rep from * to last st, K1.
**Next row:** Using yarn A, knit.
**Next row:** Using yarn A, K4, P to last 4 sts, K4.
Rep last 2 rows once more.
**Next row (RS):** Using yarn B, K1, (K1, yfwd, K1) all into next st, *sl 1, (K1, yfwd, K1) all into next st; rep from * to last st, K1.
**Next row:** Using yarn B, K1, K3tog tbl, *sl 1, K3tog tbl, rep from * to last st, K1.
Cast off using yarn A.
See information page for finishing instructions, setting in sleeves using the set-in method.

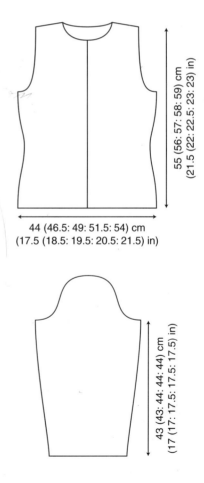

55 (56: 57: 58: 59) cm
(21.5 (22: 22.5: 23: 23) in)

44 (46.5: 49: 51.5: 54) cm
(17.5 (18.5: 19.5: 20.5: 21.5) in)

43 (43: 44: 44: 44) cm
(17 (17: 17.5: 17.5: 17.5) in)

## No 3

# ERIN

KIM HARGREAVES

## YARN

|  | XS | S | M | L | XL |  |
|---|---|---|---|---|---|---|
| To fit bust | 81 | 86 | 91 | 97 | 102 | cm |
|  | 32 | 34 | 36 | 38 | 40 | in |

**Rowan Ribbon Twist**

|  | 7 | 7 | 8 | 8 | 9 | x 100gm |

(photographed in Rocky 113)

## NEEDLES

1 pair 10mm (no 000) (US 15) needles
1 pair 12mm (US 17) needles

## TENSION

7 sts and 12 rows to 10 cm measured over moss stitch using 12mm (US 17) needles.

## BACK

Cast on 31 (33: 35: 37: 39) sts using 10mm (US 15) needles.
**Row 1 (RS):** K1, *P1, K1, rep from * to end.
**Row 2:** P1, *K1, P1, rep from * to end.
These 2 rows form rib.
Cont in rib for a further 10 rows, dec 1 st at each end of 5th of these rows and ending with a WS row. 29 (31: 33: 35: 37) sts.
Change to 12mm (US 17) needles.
**Row 13 (RS):** P2tog, K1, *P1, K1, rep from * to last 2 sts, P2tog. 27 (29: 31: 33: 35) sts.
**Row 14:** P1, *K1, P1, rep from * to end.
Last 2 rows form moss st and cont side seam shaping.
Cont in moss st, dec 1 st at each end of 5th and foll 6th row. 23 (25: 27: 29: 31) sts.
Work 5 rows, ending with a WS row.
Inc 1 st at each end of next and every foll 6th row until there are 29 (31: 33: 35: 37) sts, taking inc sts into moss st.
Cont straight until back measures 39 (40: 40: 41: 41) cm, ending with a WS row.

## Shape armholes

Keeping moss st correct, cast off 2 sts at beg of next 2 rows.
25 (27: 29: 31: 33) sts.
Dec 1 st at each end of next 2 (2: 3: 3: 4) rows.
21 (23: 23: 25: 25) sts.
Cont straight until armhole measures 20 (20: 21: 21: 22) cm, ending with a WS row.

## Shape shoulders and back neck

**Next row (RS):** Cast off 2 (3: 3: 3: 3) sts, moss st until there are 5 sts on right needle and turn, leaving rem sts on a holder.
Work each side of neck separately.
Cast off 2 sts at beg of next row.
Cast off rem 3 sts.
With RS facing, rejoin yarn to rem sts, cast off centre 7 (7: 7: 9: 9) sts, moss st to end.
Complete to match first side, reversing shapings.

## FRONT

Work as given for back until 6 (6: 6: 8: 8) rows less have been worked than on back to start of shoulder shaping, ending with a WS row.

## Shape neck

**Next row (RS):** Moss st 8 (9: 9: 10: 10) sts and turn, leaving rem sts on a holder.
Work each side of neck separately.
Dec 1 st at neck edge of next 2 rows, then on foll 1 (1: 1: 2: 2) alt rows.
5 (6: 6: 6: 6) sts.
Work 1 row, ending with a WS row

## Shape shoulder

Cast off 2 (3: 3: 3: 3) sts at beg of next row.
Work 1 row.
Cast off rem 3 sts.
With RS facing, rejoin yarn to rem sts, cast off centre 5 sts, moss st to end.
Complete to match first side, reversing shapings.

SLEEVES (both alike)

Cast on 23 sts using 10mm (US 15) needles.

**Row 1 (RS):** P1, *K1, P1, rep from * to end.

**Row 2:** K1, *P1, K1, rep from * to end.

These 2 rows form rib.

Cont in rib, dec 1 st at each end of 5th and foll 8th row. 19 sts.

Work in rib for a further 5 rows, ending with a WS row. (20 rows of rib completed.)

Change to 12mm (US 17) needles.

**Row 21 (RS):** K1, *P1, K1, rep from * to end.

**Row 22:** As row 21.

Last 2 rows form moss st.

Cont in moss st, shaping sides by inc 1 st at each end of 11th (11th: 11th: 11th: 9th) and every foll 16th (16th: 10th: 10th: 8th) row until there are 23 (23: 25: 25: 27) sts, taking inc sts into moss st.

Cont straight until sleeve measures 50 (50: 51: 51: 51) cm, ending with a WS row.

**Shape top**

Cast off 2 sts at beg of next 2 rows.

19 (19: 21: 21: 23) sts.

Dec 1 st at each end of next and every foll 4th row to 11 (11: 13: 13: 15) sts, then on foll 1 (1: 2: 2: 3) alt rows, then on foll row, ending with a WS row.

Cast off rem 7 sts.

MAKING UP

**PRESS** as described on the information page.

Join right shoulder seam using back stitch, or mattress stitch if preferred.

**Neckband**

With RS facing and using 10mm (US 15) needles, pick up and knit 8 (8: 8: 10: 10) sts down left side of neck, 7 sts from front, 8 (8: 8: 10: 10) sts up right side of neck, then 16 (16: 16: 18: 18) sts from back. 39 (39: 39: 45: 45) sts.

Beg with row 2, work in rib as given for back for 10 cm.

Cast off in rib.

See information page for finishing instructions, setting in sleeves using the set-in method.

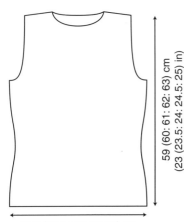

41.5 (44.5: 47: 50: 53) cm
(16.5 (17.5: 18.5: 19.5: 21) in)

59 (60: 61: 62: 63) cm
(23 (23.5: 24: 24.5: 25) in)

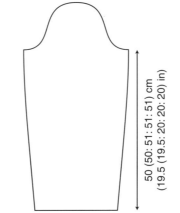

50 (50: 51: 51: 51) cm
(19.5 (19.5: 20: 20: 20) in)

No 4

# NANCY

KIM HARGREAVES

## YARN

|  | XS | S | M | L | XL |  |
|---|---|---|---|---|---|---|
| To fit bust | 81 | 86 | 91 | 97 | 102 | cm |
|  | 32 | 34 | 36 | 38 | 40 | in |

**Rowan Ribbon Twist**

| | 9 | 9 | 10 | 10 | 11 | x 100gm |

(photographed in Rabble 118)

## NEEDLES

1 pair 10mm (no 000) (US 15) needles
1 pair 12mm (US 17) needles

## TENSION

8 sts and 11 rows to 10 cm measured over stocking stitch using 12mm (US 17) needles.

## BACK

Cast on 38 (40: 42: 44: 46) sts using 10mm (US 15) needles.
**Rows 1 to 4:** Purl.
Change to 12mm (US 17) needles.
Beg with a K row, work in st st for 8 rows, ending with a WS row.
**Next row (RS):** K2, K2tog, K to last 4 sts, K2tog tbl, K2.
Working all side seam decreases as set by last row, cont in st st, dec 1 st at each end of every foll 6th row until 32 (34: 36: 38: 40) sts rem.
Cont straight until back measures 28 (29: 29: 30: 30) cm, ending with a WS row.
**Next row (RS):** K2, M1, K to last 2 sts, M1, K2.
Working all side seam increases as set by last row, inc 1 st at each end of every foll 6th row until there are 38 (40: 42: 44: 46) sts.
Work 5 rows, ending with a WS row.
**Shape armholes**
Cast off 2 sts at beg of next 2 rows.
34 (36: 38: 40: 42) sts.

Dec 1 st at each end of next 3 rows, then on foll 1 (1: 2: 2: 3) alt rows.
26 (28: 28: 30: 30) sts.
Cont straight until armhole measures 20 (20: 21: 21: 22) cm, ending with a WS row.
**Shape shoulders and back neck**
**Next row (RS):** Cast off 3 (4: 4: 4: 4) sts, K until there are 5 sts on right needle and turn, leaving rem sts on a holder.
Cast off 2 sts at beg of next row.
Cast off rem 3 sts.
With RS facing, rejoin yarn to rem sts, cast off centre 10 (10: 10: 12: 12) sts, K to end.
Complete to match first side, reversing shapings.

## LEFT FRONT

Cast on 30 (31: 32: 33: 34) sts using 10mm (US 15) needles.
**Row 1 (RS):** P to last 7 sts, K7.
**Row 2:** K1, (take yarn round needle and draw loop through st on right needle as though to K a st) 4 times (to create short chain), K6, P to end.
**Rows 3 and 4:** As rows 1 and 2.
Change to 12mm (US 17) needles.
**Row 5 (RS):** Knit.
**Row 6:** K1, (take yarn round needle and draw loop through st on right needle as though to K a st) 4 times (to create short chain), K6, P to end.
Last 2 rows set the sts – front opening edge 7 sts as fancy edging and rem sts in st st.
Keeping sts correct as set, work 6 rows, ending with a WS row.
Working all side seam decreases as given for back, dec 1 st at beg of next and every foll 6th row until 27 (28: 29: 30: 31) sts rem.
Cont straight until 4 rows less have been worked than on back to first side seam inc, ending with a WS row.

**Shape front slope**

**Next row (RS):** K to last 10 sts, K2tog tbl, K8.
26 (27: 28: 29: 30) sts.

**Next row:** K1, (take yarn round needle and draw loop through st on right needle as though to K a st) 4 times (to create short chain), K6, wrap next st (by slipping next st to right needle, taking yarn to opposite side of work between needles and then slipping same st back onto left needle – when working back across sts work the wrapped loop tog with the wrapped st), turn, K7, turn, K1, (take yarn round needle and draw loop through st on right needle as though to K a st) 4 times (to create short chain), K6, P to end.

**Next row:** K to last 10 (10: 0: 10: 10) sts, (K2tog tbl, K8) 1 (1: 0: 1: 1) times.
25 (26: 28: 28: 29) sts.

**Next row:** K1, (take yarn round needle and draw loop through st on right needle as though to K a st) 4 times (to create short chain), K6, P to end.

Last 4 rows set the sts, and front slope decreases – front opening edge 7 sts as frill edging and rem sts in st st.

Working all front slope decreases as now set and side seam increases as set by back, dec 1 st at front slope edge of 3rd (3rd: next: next: next) and 3 (3: 4: 4: 4) foll 4th rows **and at same time** inc 1 st at side seam edge on next and 2 foll 6th rows.
24 (25: 26: 26: 27) sts.

Work 3 (3: 1: 1: 1) rows, ending with a WS row. (Left front now matches back to beg of armhole shaping.)

**Shape armhole**

Keeping sts correct, cast off 2 sts at beg and dec 1 (1: 0: 0: 0) st at front slope edge of next row.
21 (22: 24: 24: 25) sts.

Work 1 row.

Dec 1 st at armhole edge of next 3 rows, then on foll 1 (1: 2: 2: 3) alt rows **and at same time** dec 1 st at front slope edge of 3rd (3rd: next: next: next) and every foll 0 (0: 4th: 4th: 4th) row.
16 (17: 17: 17: 16) sts.

Dec 1 st at front slope edge **only** on 2nd (2nd: 2nd: 2nd: 4th) and every foll 4th row until 13 (14: 14: 14: 14) sts rem.

Cont straight until left front matches back to start of shoulder shaping, ending with a WS row.

**Shape shoulder**

Cast off 3 (4: 4: 4: 4) sts at beg of next row, then 2 sts at beg of foll alt row. 8 sts.

Cont as set on these 8 sts until shorter edge measures 9 (9: 9: 10: 10) cm. Cast off.

RIGHT FRONT

Cast on 30 (31: 32: 33: 34) sts using 10mm (US 15) needles.

**Row 1 (RS):** K7, P to end.

**Row 2:** P to last 7 sts, K7.

**Row 3:** K1, (take yarn round needle and draw loop through st on right needle as though to K a st) 4 times (to create short chain), K6, P to end.

**Row 4:** As row 2.

Change to 12mm (US 17) needles.

**Row 5 (RS):** K1, (take yarn round needle and draw loop through st on right needle as though to K a st) 4 times (to create short chain), K to end.

**Row 6:** P to last 7 sts, K7.

Last 2 rows set the sts – front opening edge 7 sts as fancy edging and rem sts in st st.

Keeping sts correct as set, work 6 rows, ending with a WS row.

Working all side seam decreases as given for back, dec 1 st at end of next and every foll 6th row until 27 (28: 29: 30: 31) sts rem.

Cont straight until 4 rows less have been worked than on back to first side seam inc, ending with a WS row.

**Shape front slope**

**Next row (RS):** K1, (take yarn round needle and draw loop through st on right needle as though to K a st) 4 times (to create short chain), K6, wrap next st, turn, K7, turn, K1, (take yarn round needle and draw loop through st on right needle as though to K a st) 4 times (to create short chain), K7, K2tog, K to end. 26 (27: 28: 29: 30) sts.

**Next row:** P to last 7 sts, K7.

**Next row:** K1, (take yarn round needle and draw loop through st on right needle as though to K a st) 4 times (to create short chain), (K7, K2tog) 1 (1: 0: 1: 1) times, K to end. 25 (26: 28: 28: 29) sts.

**Next row:** P to last 7 sts, K7.

Last 4 rows set the sts, and front slope decreases – front opening edge 7 sts as frill edging and rem sts in st st.

Complete to match left front, reversing shapings.

## SLEEVES (both alike)

Cast on 22 sts using 12mm (US 17) needles.

Beg with a K row, work in st st for 14 (14: 8: 8: 4) rows, ending with a WS row.

**Next row (RS):** K2, M1, K to last 2 sts, M1, K2. Working all increases as set by last row, inc 1 st at each end of every foll 14th (14th: 10th: 10th: 8th) row until there are 26 (26: 28: 28: 30) sts.

Cont straight until sleeve measures 35 (35: 36: 36: 36) cm, ending with a WS row.

### Shape top

Cast off 2 sts at beg of next 2 rows.

22 (22: 24: 24: 26) sts.

Dec 1 st at each end of next and foll alt row, then on every foll 4th row to 14 (14: 16: 16: 18) sts, then on foll 1 (1: 2: 2: 3) alt rows, then on foll row, ending with a WS row. Cast off rem 10 sts.

## MAKING UP

**PRESS** as described on the information page. Join both shoulder seams using back stitch, or mattress stitch if preferred.

Join cast-off ends of frill strips, then sew shorter edge to back neck, easing in fullness.

### Cuffs (both alike)

Cast on 8 sts using 12mm (US 17) needles.

**Rows 1 and 2:** Knit.

**Row 3 (RS):** K1, (take yarn round needle and draw loop through st on right needle as though to K a st) 4 times (to create short chain), K6, wrap next st, turn, K7, turn, K1, (take yarn round needle and draw loop through st on right needle as though to K a st) 4 times (to create short chain), K to end.

**Row 4:** Knit.

**Row 5:** K1, (take yarn round needle and draw loop through st on right needle as though to K a st) 4 times (to create short chain), K to end.

**Row 6:** Knit.

Rep last 4 rows until shorter edge of cuff fits along cast-on edge of sleeve, ending with a WS row.

Cast off.

Sew cuffs to lower edges of sleeves.

See information page for finishing instructions, setting in sleeves using the set-in method.

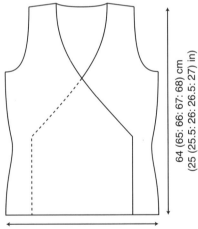

64 (65: 66: 67: 68) cm
(25 (25.5: 26: 26.5: 27) in)

35 (35: 36: 36: 36) cm (14 in)

47.5 (50: 52.5: 55: 57.5) cm
(18.5 (19.5: 20.5: 21.5: 22.5) in)

No 5

# Casey

KIM HARGREAVES

## YARN

**Rowan Ribbon Twist**

  3     x     100gm

(photographed in Riddler 112)

## NEEDLES

1 pair 15mm (US 19) needles

Cable needle

## TENSION

7 sts and 8 rows to 10 cm measured over stocking stitch using 15mm (US 19) needles.

## FINISHED SIZE

Completed scarf measures 13 cm (5 in) wide and 183 cm (72 in) long.

## SPECIAL ABBREVIATIONS

**C8B =** slip next 4 sts onto cable needle and leave at back of work, K4, then K4 from cable needle.

**C8F =** slip next 4 sts onto cable needle and leave at front of work, K4, then K4 from cable needle.

**MB =** make bobble as folls: (K1, yfwd, K1, yfwd, K1) all into next st, turn, K5, turn, P5, turn, K5, turn, slip next 2 sts, K3tog, pass 2 slipped sts over – bobble completed.

## SCARF

**Border**

Cast on 14 sts using 15mm (US 19) needles.

Border patt as folls:

**Row 1 (RS):** K1, C8B, K5.

**Row 2 and every foll alt row:** K1, P12, K1.

**Row 3:** K9, MB, K4.

**Row 5:** K14.

**Row 7:** K5, C8F, K1.

**Row 9:** K4, MB, K9.

**Row 11:** K14.

**Row 12:** As row 2.

These 12 rows form border patt.

**Main section**

Work in border patt for a further 12 rows, ending with a WS row.

Now work in main patt as folls:

**Row 1 (RS):** K1, C8B, K5.

**Row 2 and every foll alt row:** K1, P12, K1.

**Rows 3 and 5:** K14.

**Row 7:** K5, C8F, K1.

**Rows 9 and 11:** K14.

**Row 12:** As row 2.

These 12 rows form main patt.

Cont in main patt until scarf measures approx 150 cm, ending after main patt row 12.

**Border**

Beg with border patt row 1, work in border patt for 26 rows, ending with a WS row.

Cast off.

## MAKING UP

**PRESS** as described on the information page.

No 6

# NORA

KIM HARGREAVES

**YARN**

| | | XS | S | M | L | XL | |
|---|---|---|---|---|---|---|---|
| To fit bust | | 81 | 86 | 91 | 97 | 102 | cm |
| | | 32 | 34 | 36 | 38 | 40 | in |

**Rowan Ribbon Twist and Big Wool Tuft**

| A Twist | Riches | 116 | 8 | 9 | 9 | 10 | 10 | x 100gm |
| B Tuft | Frosty | 055 | 2 | 2 | 2 | 2 | 2 | x 50gm |

**NEEDLES**

1 pair 10mm (no 000) (US 15) needles
1 pair 12mm (US 17) needles

**TENSION**

8 sts and 11 rows to 10 cm measured over stocking stitch using 12mm (US 17) needles.

BACK

Cast on 35 (37: 39: 41: 43) sts using 10mm (US 15) needles and yarn A.
**Rows 1 and 2:** Purl.
Change to 12mm (US 17) needles.
Beg with a K row, work in st st for 4 rows.
**Row 7 (dec) (RS):** K2, K2tog, K to last 4 sts, K2tog tbl, K2.
Working all decreases as set by last row, dec 1 st at each end of 4th and foll 4th row.
29 (31: 33: 35: 37) sts.
Work 5 rows, ending with a WS row.
**Next row (inc) (RS):** K2, M1, K to last 2 sts, M1, K2.
Working all increases as set by last row, inc 1 st at each end of 6th and foll 6th row.
35 (37: 39: 41: 43) sts.
Cont straight until back measures 35 (36: 36: 37: 37) cm, ending with a WS row.
**Shape armholes**
Cast off 2 sts at beg of next 2 rows.
31 (33: 35: 37: 39) sts.

Dec 1 st at each end of next 2 (2: 3: 3: 4) rows.
27 (29: 29: 31: 31) sts.
Cont straight until armhole measures 20 (20: 21: 21: 22) cm, ending with a WS row.
**Shape shoulders and back neck**
**Next row (RS):** Cast off 3 (4: 4: 4: 4) sts, K until there are 5 sts on right needle and turn, leaving rem sts on a holder.
Work each side of neck separately.
Cast off 2 sts at beg of next row.
Cast off rem 3 sts.
With RS facing, rejoin yarn to rem sts, cast off centre 11 (11: 11: 13: 13) sts, K to end.
Complete to match first side, reversing shapings.

FRONT

Work as given for back until 6 (6: 6: 8: 8) rows less have been worked than on back to start of shoulder shaping, ending with a WS row.
**Shape neck**
**Next row (RS):** K10 (11: 11: 12: 12) and turn, leaving rem sts on a holder.
Work each side of neck separately.
Dec 1 st at neck edge of next 3 rows, then on foll 1 (1: 1: 2: 2) alt rows, ending with a WS row.
6 (7: 7: 7: 7) sts.
**Shape shoulder**
Cast off 3 (4: 4: 4: 4) sts at beg of next row.
Work 1 row.
Cast off rem 3 sts.
With RS facing, rejoin yarn to rem sts, cast off centre 7 sts, K to end.
Complete to match first side, reversing shapings.

SLEEVES (both alike)

Cast on 25 sts using 12mm (US 17) needles and yarn A.
Join in yarn B.

**Row 1 (RS):** Using yarn B, K1, (K1, yfwd, K1) all into next st, *sl 1, (K1, yfwd, K1) all into next st; rep from * to last st, K1.

**Row 2:** Using yarn B, K1, K3tog tbl, *sl 1, K3tog tbl, rep from * to last st, K1.

**Row 3:** Using yarn A, knit.

**Row 4:** Using yarn A, purl.

**Rows 5 and 6:** As rows 3 and 4.

**Row 7:** Using yarn B, K2tog, (K1, yfwd, K1) all into next st, *sl 1, (K1, yfwd, K1) all into next st; rep from * to last 2 sts, K2tog. 23 sts.

**Row 8:** As row 2.

Break off yarn B and cont using yarn A only.

Beg with a K row, work in st st for 14 rows, dec 1 st at each end of 3rd of these rows and ending with a WS row. 21 sts.

**Row 23 (inc) (RS):** K2, M1, K to last 2 sts, M1, K2. 23 sts.

Working all increases as set by last row, inc 1 st at each end of every foll 10th (10th: 6th: 6th: 4th) row to 27 sts, then on every foll − (−: 8th: 8th: 6th) row until there are − (−: 29: 29: 31) sts.

Cont straight until sleeve measures 43 (43: 44: 44: 44) cm, ending with a WS row.

**Shape top**

Cast off 2 sts at beg of next 2 rows.

23 (23: 25: 25: 27) sts.

Dec 1 st at each end of next and foll alt row, then on foll 4th row, then on every foll alt row to 11 sts, then on foll row, ending with a WS row.

Cast off rem 9 sts.

MAKING UP

**PRESS** as described on the information page.

Join both shoulder seams using back stitch, or mattress stitch if preferred.

**Collar**

Cast on 20 sts using 12mm (US 17) needles and yarn A.

Beg with a K row, work in st st for 2 rows, ending with a WS row.

Join in yarn B.

**Row 1 (RS):** Using yarn A, K8, using yarn B, (K1, yfwd, K1) all into next st, *sl 1, (K1, yfwd, K1) all into next st; rep from * to last st, K1.

**Row 2:** Using yarn B, K1, K3tog tbl, (sl 1, K3tog tbl) 5 times, turn.

**Row 3:** Using yarn A, K12.

**Row 4:** Using yarn A, P to end.

**Row 5:** Using yarn A, K to end.

**Row 6:** As row 4.

These 6 rows form patt.

Cont in patt until shorter edge of collar fits around neck edge, ending after patt row 6 and a WS row.

Cast off.

Join cast-on and cast-off ends of collar. Placing collar seam at centre back neck, sew shorter edge of collar to neck edge.

See information page for finishing instructions, setting in sleeves using the set-in method.

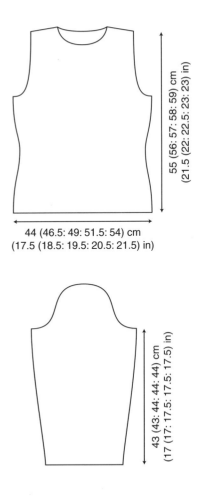

55 (56: 57: 58: 59) cm
(21.5 (22: 22.5: 23: 23) in)

44 (46.5: 49: 51.5: 54) cm
(17.5 (18.5: 19.5: 20.5: 21.5) in)

43 (43: 44: 44: 44) cm
(17 (17: 17.5: 17.5: 17.5) in)

No 7

# EBONY

KIM HARGREAVES

## YARN

|  | XS | S | M | L | XL |  |
|---|---|---|---|---|---|---|
| To fit bust | 81 | 86 | 91 | 97 | 102 | cm |
|  | 32 | 34 | 36 | 38 | 40 | in |

**Rowan Ribbon Twist**

|  | 4 | 4 | 5 | 6 | 6 | x 100gm |

(photographed in Ripple 114)

## NEEDLES

1 pair 10mm (no 000) (US 15) needles
1 pair 12mm (US 17) needles

**FASTENER** – 1 decorative pin or brooch

## TENSION

8 sts and 11 rows to 10 cm measured over stocking stitch using 12mm (US 17) needles.

## CAPE

Cast on 124 (132: 140: 148: 156) sts using 10mm (US 15) needles.
**Row 1 (WS):** K2, P to last 2 sts, K2.
**Row 2:** K2, ★(K2tog) twice, (yfwd) twice, (sl 1, K1, psso) twice, rep from ★ to last 2 sts, K2.
**Row 3:** K2, ★P2tog tbl, (P1, K1) 3 times into double yfwd of previous row, P2tog, rep from ★ to last 2 sts, K2.
**Row 4:** K3, ★K6, K2tog but do NOT slip sts off left needle, K first of these 2 sts again and let sts fall off left needle, rep from ★ to last 9 sts, K9.
**Row 5:** As row 1.
**Row 6:** K6, ★(K2tog) twice, (yfwd) twice, (sl 1, K1, psso) twice, rep from ★ to last 6 sts, K6.
**Row 7:** K2, P4, ★P2tog tbl, (P1, K1) 3 times into double yfwd of previous row, P2tog, rep from ★ to last 6 sts, P4, K2.
**Row 8:** K5, ★K2tog but do NOT slip sts off left needle, K first of these 2 sts again and let sts fall off

left needle, K6, rep from ★ to last 7 sts, K2tog but do NOT slip sts off left needle, K first of these 2 sts again and let sts fall off left needle, K5.
**Rows 9 to 12:** As rows 1 to 4.
**Row 13 (WS):** K2, (P2tog tbl, P2) 7 (6: 5: 4: 3) times, (P2tog tbl, P1) 2 (6: 10: 14: 18) times, (P2tog tbl, P2) 6 (5: 4: 3: 2) times, P2tog tbl, P2tog, (P2, P2tog) 6 (5: 4: 3: 2) times, (P1, P2tog) 2 (6: 10: 14: 18) times, (P2, P2tog) 7 (6: 5: 4: 3) times, K2. 92 (96: 100: 104: 108) sts.
**Row 14 (RS):** Knit.
**Row 15:** K2, P to last 2 sts, K2.
Last 2 rows form patt.
Cont in patt until cape measures 16 cm, ending with a WS row.
**Shape shoulders**
Place markers after 24th (25th: 26th: 27th: 28th) st, counting in from both ends of last row.
**Next row (dec) (RS):** (K to within 2 sts of marker, K2tog, slip marker to right needle, K2tog tbl) twice, K to end. 88 (92: 96: 100: 104) sts.
Work 3 rows.
Rep last 4 rows twice more, then first of these rows (the dec row) again. 76 (80: 84: 88: 92) sts.
Work 1 row, ending with a WS row.

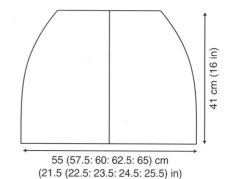

55 (57.5: 60: 62.5: 65) cm
(21.5 (22.5: 23.5: 24.5: 25.5) in)

41 cm (16 in)

Change to 10mm (US 15) needles.
**Next row (RS):** K1 (1: 0: 0: 0), (K2, K2tog tbl)
5 (4: 5: 4: 4) times, (K1, K2tog tbl) 0 (1: 1: 2: 3) times,
(K1, K2tog) 0 (2: 1: 2: 3) times, (K2, K2tog) 4 (3: 4:
4: 3) times, K2 (4: 0: 0: 0), (K2tog tbl, K2) 4 (3: 4: 4:
3) times, (K2tog tbl, K1) 0 (2: 1: 2: 3) times, (K2tog,
K1) 0 (1: 1: 2: 3) times, (K2tog, K2) 5 (4: 5: 4: 4)
times, K1 (1: 0: 0: 0). 58 (60: 62: 64: 66) sts.

Work 3 rows.
Change to 12mm (US 17) needles.
Work a further 10 rows, ending with a WS row.
Cast off.

MAKING UP
**PRESS** as described on the information page.
Fasten neck with decorative pin.

No 8

# ALPHA

KIM HARGREAVES

YARN
One size
**Rowan Ribbon Twist**
   1   x   100gm
(photographed in Racy 117)

NEEDLES
1 pair 10mm (no 000) (US 15) needles
1 pair 12mm (US 17) needles

TENSION
8 sts and 11 rows to 10 cm measured over stocking
stitch using 12mm (US 17) needles.

HAT
Cast on 7 sts using 12mm (US 17) needles.
**Row 1 (WS):** P7.
**Row 2:** (K1, M1) 6 times, K1. 13 sts.
**Row 3:** P1, (M1P, P2) 6 times. 19 sts.
**Row 4:** (K3, M1) 6 times, K1. 25 sts.
**Row 5:** Purl.
**Row 6:** (K4, M1) 6 times, K1. 31 sts.
Beg with a P row, work in st st for 3 rows.

**Row 10:** (K5, M1) 6 times, K1. 37 sts.
Beg with a P row, work in st st for 9 rows, ending
with a WS row.
Change to 10mm (US 15) needles.
Work in garter st for 6 rows, ending with a WS row.
**Shape for earflaps**
**Next row (RS):** Cast off 4 sts, K until there are
9 sts on right needle and slip these sts onto a holder,
cast off next 11 sts, K until there are 9 sts on right
needle, cast off rem 4 sts.
With **WS** facing, rejoin yarn to last set of 9 sts and
cont as folls:
Work in garter st for 3 rows, ending with a WS row.
Cont in garter st, dec 1 st at each end of next and
foll 4th row, then on foll alt row. 3 sts.
Work 1 row.
**Next row (RS):** K3tog and fasten off.
With **WS** facing, rejoin yarn to other set of 9 sts and
complete second earflap to match first.

MAKING UP
**PRESS** as described on the information page.
Join back seam.

No 9

# JOSIE

KIM HARGREAVES

## YARN
**Rowan Ribbon Twist**
   3     x     100gm
(photographed in Ribble 111)

## NEEDLES
1 pair 12mm (US 17) needles
Cable needle

## TENSION
8 sts and 11 rows to 10 cm measured over stocking
stitch using 12mm (US 17) needles.

## FINISHED SIZE
Completed bag measures 25 cm (10 in) wide and
31 cm (12 in) deep.

## SPECIAL ABBREVIATIONS
**C8B =** slip next 4 sts onto cable needle and leave
at back of work, K4, then K4 from cable needle.
**C8F =** slip next 4 sts onto cable needle and leave at
front of work, K4, then K4 from cable needle.

## BAG
Cast on 19 sts using 12mm (US 17) needles.
Beg with a K row, work in st st for 8 rows, ending
with a WS row.
**Row 9 (eyelet row) (RS):** (K1, K2tog, yfwd)
6 times, K1.
Work in st st for a further 3 rows, ending with a
WS row.
**Row 13 (inc) (RS):** K1, (M1, K2) 9 times. 28 sts.
Cont in patt as folls:
**Row 1 and every foll alt row:** Purl.
**Row 2:** Knit.
**Row 4:** K2, C8F, K4, C8F, K6.

**Rows 6 and 8:** Knit.
**Row 10:** K6, C8B, K4, C8B, K2.
**Row 12:** Knit.
These 12 rows form patt.
Cont in patt for a further 43 rows, ending with a
WS row.
**Next row (dec) (RS):** K1, (K2tog, K1) 9 times.
19 sts.
Beg with a P row, work in st st for 3 rows, ending
with a WS row.
**Next row (eyelet row) (RS):** (K1, K2tog, yfwd)
6 times, K1.
Work in st st for a further 8 rows.
Cast off purlwise (on WS).

## HANDLES (make 2)
Cast on 9 sts using 12mm (US 17) needles.
**Row 1 (RS):** K2, sl 1 purlwise (for fold line), K3,
sl 1 purlwise (for fold line), K2.
**Row 2:** Purl.
Rep last 2 rows 19 times more.
Cast off.

## MAKING UP
**PRESS** as described on the information page.
Fold bag in half and join row-end edges to form
side seams. Fold first and last 6 rows to inside
around opening edge and stitch in place. Fold
handles in half along fold lines and stitch row-end
edges together. Positioning handles 5 cm apart,
attach ends of handles to inside of opening edge,
making sure outer layer of knitting is left free.
Make a 100 cm long twisted cord and thread
through eyelet rows around top of bag. Make two
7 cm diameter pompoms and attach one to each
end of twisted cord.

# No 10

# BETH

KIM HARGREAVES

## YARN

|  | XS | S | M | L | XL |  |
|---|---|---|---|---|---|---|
| To fit bust | 81 | 86 | 91 | 97 | 102 | cm |
|  | 32 | 34 | 36 | 38 | 40 | in |

**Rowan Ribbon Twist**

|  | 8 | 8 | 8 | 9 | 9 | x 100gm |

(photographed in Rapid 115)

## NEEDLES
1 pair 12mm (US 17) needles

## TENSION
8 sts and 11 rows to 10 cm measured over stocking stitch using 12mm (US 17) needles.

**Pattern note**: As row end edges form actual finished front neck opening edges of garment, it is important these edges are kept neat. Therefore avoid joining in new balls of yarn at these edges.

## BACK
Cast on 36 (38: 40: 42: 44) sts using 12mm (US 17) needles.
**Rows 1 to 8:** Purl.
Beg with a K row, work in st st for 6 rows, ending with a WS row.
**Row 15 (dec) (RS):** K2, K2tog, K to last 4 sts, K2tog tbl, K2. 34 (36: 38: 40: 42) sts.
Work in st st for a further 7 rows.
**Row 23:** As row 15.
32 (34: 36: 38: 40) sts.
Cont in st st until back measures 28 (29: 29: 30: 30) cm, ending with RS facing for next row.
**Next row (inc) (RS):** K2, M1, K to last 2 sts, M1, K2. 34 (36: 38: 40: 42) sts.★★
Work 9 rows, then rep the inc row again.
36 (38: 40: 42: 44) sts.
Work a further 5 rows, ending with a WS row.

**Shape armholes**
Cast off 2 sts at beg of next 2 rows.
32 (34: 36: 38: 40) sts.
Dec 1 st at each end of next 3 (3: 4: 4: 5) rows.
26 (28: 28: 30: 30) sts.
Cont straight until armhole measures 20 (20: 21: 21: 22) cm, ending with a WS row.
**Shape shoulders**
Cast off 3 (4: 4: 4: 4) sts at beg of next 2 rows, then 3 sts at beg of foll 2 rows.
Leave rem 14 (14: 14: 16: 16) sts on a holder.

## FRONT
Work as given for back to ★★.
Work 6 rows, ending with a **RS** row.
**Next row (WS):** P16 (17: 18: 19: 20), K2, P to end.
**Next row:** Knit.
**Next row:** P15 (16: 17: 18: 19), K4, P to end.
**Divide for front opening**
**Next row (RS):** K2, M1, K15 (16: 17: 18: 19) and turn, leaving rem sts on a holder.
18 (19: 20: 21: 22) sts.
Work each side of neck separately.
**Next row (WS):** K2, P to end.
**Next row:** Knit.
These 2 rows set the sts – front opening edge 2 sts in garter st with all other sts in st st.
Keeping sts correct as set, work a further 3 rows, ending with a WS row. (Front should now match back to beg of armhole shaping.)
**Shape armhole**
Cast off 2 sts at beg of next row.
16 (17: 18: 19: 20) sts.
Work 1 row.
Dec 1 st at armhole edge of next 3 (3: 4: 4: 4) rows.
13 (14: 14: 15: 16) sts.
Work 1 (1: 0: 0: 0) rows, ending with a WS row.

**Next row (RS):** (K2tog) 0 (0: 0: 0: 1) times, K to last 4 sts, K2tog tbl, K2. 12 (13: 13: 14: 14) sts.
Cont straight until front matches back to start of shoulder shaping, ending with a WS row.

### Shape shoulder
Cast off 3 (4: 4: 4: 4) sts at beg of next row, then 3 sts at beg of foll alt row.
Work 1 row, ending with a WS row.
Leave rem 6 (6: 6: 7: 7) sts on a holder.
With RS facing, rejoin yarn to rem sts, K to last 2 sts, M1, K2. 18 (19: 20: 21: 22) sts.

**Next row (WS):** P to last 2 sts, K2.

**Next row:** Knit.
These 2 rows set the sts – front opening edge 2 sts in garter st with all other sts in st st.
Keeping sts correct as set, work a further 4 rows, ending with a RS row. (Front should now match back to beg of armhole shaping.)

### Shape armhole
Cast off 2 sts at beg of next row. 16 (17: 18: 19: 20) sts.
Dec 1 st at armhole edge of next 3 (3: 4: 4: 4) rows.
13 (14: 14: 15: 16) sts.
Work 1 (1: 0: 0: 0) rows, ending with a WS row.

**Next row (RS):** K2, K2tog, K to last 0 (0: 0: 0: 2) sts, (K2tog) 0 (0: 0: 0: 1) times.
12 (13: 13: 14: 14) sts.
Cont straight until front matches back to start of shoulder shaping, ending with a RS row.

### Shape shoulder
Cast off 3 (4: 4: 4: 4) sts at beg of next row, then 3 sts at beg of foll alt row, ending with a WS row.
Leave rem 6 (6: 6: 7: 7) sts on a holder – do NOT break yarn but set this ball of yarn to one side for collar.

### SLEEVES (both alike)
Cast on 26 sts using 12mm (US 17) needles.

**Rows 1 to 6:** Purl.

**Row 7 (RS):** P2, P2tog, P to last 4 sts, P2tog tbl, P2. 24 sts.

**Rows 8 to 10:** Purl.

**Row 11 (RS):** K2, K2tog, K to last 4 sts, K2tog tbl, K2. 22 sts.
Beg with a P row, work in st st for 3 rows.

**Row 15:** As row 11. 20 sts.
Work in st st for a further 7 rows, end with a WS row.

**Row 23 (inc) (RS):** K2, M1, K to last 2 sts, M1, K2. 22 sts.

Working all increases as set by last row, inc 1 st at each end of every foll 10th (10th: 6th: 6th: 4th) row to 26 sts, then on every foll – (–: 8th: 8th: 6th) row until there are – (–: 28: 28: 30) sts.
Cont straight until sleeve measures 43 (43: 44: 44: 44) cm, ending with a WS row.

### Shape top
Cast off 2 sts at beg of next 2 rows.
22 (22: 24: 24: 26) sts.
Dec 1 st at each end of next and foll alt row, then on every foll 4th row to 14 (14: 16: 16: 18) sts, then on foll 1 (1: 2: 2: 3) alt rows, then on foll row, ending with a WS row. Cast off rem 10 sts.

### MAKING UP
**PRESS** as described on the information page.
Join both shoulder seams using back stitch, or mattress stitch if preferred.

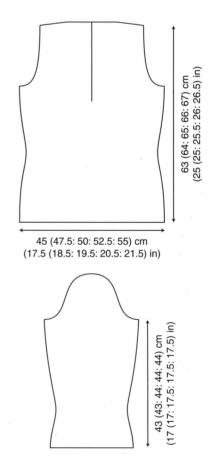

63 (64: 65: 66: 67) cm
(25 (25: 25.5: 26: 26.5) in)

45 (47.5: 50: 52.5: 55) cm
(17.5 (18.5: 19.5: 20.5: 21.5) in)

43 (43: 44: 44: 44) cm
(17 (17: 17.5: 17.5: 17.5) in)

## Collar

With RS facing, using 12mm (US 17) needles and ball of yarn left with right front, knit across 6 (6: 6: 7: 7) sts of right front, 14 (14: 14: 16: 16) sts of back, then 6 (6: 6: 7: 7) sts of left front. 26 (26: 26: 30: 30) sts.

**Next row (WS):** K2, P to last 2 sts, K2.

**Next row:** Knit.

Rep last 2 rows 4 times more.

Work in garter st for 2 rows.

Cast off knitwise (on WS).

See information page for finishing instructions, setting in sleeves using the set-in method.

# No 11

## LISSA

KIM HARGREAVES

### YARN

One size

**Rowan Ribbon Twist and Big Wool Tuft**

A Twist Rabble 118   2   x   100gm
B Tuft Rugged 058   1   x   50gm

### NEEDLES

1 pair 12mm (US 17) needles

### RIBBON

80 cm of narrow satin ribbon

### TENSION

8 sts and 11 rows to 10 cm measured over stocking stitch using 12mm (US 17) needles.

### COLLAR

Cast on 73 sts using 12mm (US 17) needles and yarn A.

Join in yarn B.

**Row 1 (RS):** Using yarn B, K1, (K1, yfwd, K1) all into next st, *sl 1, (K1, yfwd, K1) all into next st, rep from * to last st, K1.

**Row 2:** Using yarn B, K1, K3tog tbl, *sl 1, K3tog tbl, rep from * to last st, K1.

**Row 3:** Using yarn A, knit.

**Row 4:** Using yarn A, K2, P to last 2 sts, K2.

**Rows 5 and 6:** As rows 3 and 4.

**Rows 7 and 8:** As rows 1 and 2.

Break off yarn B and cont using yarn A only.

Place markers on 19th st in from each end of last row.

**Row 9:** (K to within 2 sts of marked st, K2tog tbl, K marked st, K2tog) twice, K to end. 69 sts.

**Row 10:** K2, P to last 2 sts, K2.

**Row 11:** Knit.

**Row 12:** As row 10.

**Rows 13 to 20:** As rows 9 to 12, twice. 61 sts.

**Rows 21 and 22:** As rows 9 and 10. 57 sts.

**Row 23:** As row 9. 53 sts.

**Row 24:** K2, (P to within 2 sts of marked st, P2tog, P marked st, P2tog tbl) twice, P to last 2 sts, K2.

Cast off rem 49 sts.

### MAKING UP

**PRESS** as described on the information page.

Cut ribbon into 2 equal lengths and attach one piece to each end of cast-off edge.

No 12

# CHARITY

KIM HARGREAVES

## YARN

|  | XS | S | M | L | XL |  |
|---|---|---|---|---|---|---|
| To fit bust | 81 | 86 | 91 | 97 | 102 | cm |
|  | 32 | 34 | 36 | 38 | 40 | in |

**Rowan Ribbon Twist**

|  | 7 | 7 | 8 | 8 | 9 | x 100gm |

(photographed in Ribble 111)

## NEEDLES

1 pair 8mm (no 0) (US 11) needles
1 pair 10mm (no 000) (US 15) needles
1 pair 12mm (US 17) needles

## TENSION

8 sts and 11 rows to 10 cm measured over stocking stitch using 12mm (US 17) needles.

## BACK and FRONT (both alike)

Cast on 33 (35: 37: 39: 41) sts using 10mm (US 15) needles.
**Row 1 (RS):** P1, *K1, P1, rep from * to end.
**Row 2:** K1, *P1, K1, rep from * to end.
These 2 rows form rib.
Cont in rib for a further 4 rows, ending with a WS row.
Change to 12mm (US 17) needles.
**Row 7 (dec) (RS):** K2, K2tog, K to last 4 sts, K2tog tbl, K2.
Beg with a P row, work in st st for 3 rows.
**Row 11:** As row 7. 29 (31: 33: 35: 37) sts.
Beg with a P row, work in st st for 9 rows, ending with a WS row.
**Row 21 (inc) (RS):** K2, M1, K to last 2 sts, M1, K2.
Rep last 10 rows once more.
33 (35: 37: 39: 41) sts.
Beg with a P row, cont in st st until work measures 35 (36: 36: 37: 37) cm, ending with a WS row.

## Shape armholes

Cast off 2 sts at beg of next 2 rows.
29 (31: 33: 35: 37) sts.
Dec 1 st at each end of next 3 (3: 4: 4: 5) rows.
23 (25: 25: 27: 27) sts.
Cont straight until armhole measures 12 (12: 13: 13: 14) cm, ending with a WS row.
Break yarn and leave rem 23 (25: 25: 27: 27) sts on a holder.

## SLEEVES (both alike)

Cast on 23 sts using 10mm (US 15) needles.
Work in rib as given for back and front for 10 rows, ending with a WS row.
Change to 12mm (US 17) needles.
Beg with a K row, work in st st for 16 (16: 12: 12: 10) rows, ending with a WS row.
**Next row (inc) (RS):** K2, M1, K to last 2 sts, M1, K2. 25 sts.
## M, L and XL sizes
Working all increases as set by last row, inc 1 st at each end of – (–: 12th: 12th: 10th) and foll – (–: –: –: 10th) row. – (–: 27: 27: 29) sts.
## All sizes
Cont straight until sleeve measures 46 (46: 47: 47: 47) cm, ending with a WS row.
## Shape top
Cast off 2 sts at beg of next 2 rows.
21 (21: 23: 23: 25) sts.
Dec 1 st at each end of next and every foll alt row until 7 sts rem.
Work 1 row, ending with a WS row.
Leave rem 7 sts on a holder.

## MAKING UP

**PRESS** as described on the information page.
Join both front and right back semi-raglan seams using back stitch, or mattress stitch if preferred.

## Collar

With RS facing and using 8mm (US 11) needles, work across 7 sts of left sleeve as folls: P2, K1, P1 and place marker on this st, K1, P2tog, work across 23 (25: 25: 27: 27) sts of front as folls: K2tog, P1, (K1, P1) 9 (10: 10: 11: 11) times, K2tog tbl, work across 7 sts of right sleeve as folls: P2tog, K1, P1 and place marker on this st, K1, P2tog, then work across 23 (25: 25: 27: 27) sts of back as folls: K2tog, (P1, K1) 10 (11: 11: 12: 12) times, P1.
54 (58: 58: 62: 62) sts.

**Row 1 (WS of body, RS of collar):** ★K1, P1, rep from ★ to last 2 sts, K2.

**Row 2:** P2, ★K1, P1, rep from ★ to end.

These 2 rows form rib.

Change to 10mm (US 15) needles.

Keeping rib correct, cont as folls:

**Row 3:** (Rib to within 1 st of marked st, sl 1, K2tog – marked st is first of these 2 sts, psso) twice, rib to end. 50 (54: 54: 58: 58) sts.

Work 3 rows.

**Row 7**: (Rib to within 1 st of marked st, sl 1, K2tog – marked st is first of these 2 sts, psso) twice. 46 (50: 50: 54: 54) sts.

Work 3 rows.

Change to 12mm (US 17) needles.

Work 4 rows.

**Row 15:** (Rib to marked st, M1, K marked st, M1) twice, rib to end.

Work 3 rows.

**Row 19:** As row 15. 54 (58: 58: 62: 62) sts.

Work a further 5 rows.

Cast off in rib **very loosely**.

Join left back semi-raglan and collar seam, reversing collar seam for turn-back.

See information page for finishing instructions.

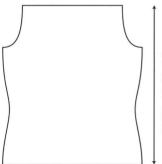

41.5 (44: 46.5: 49: 51.5) cm
(16.5 (17.5: 18.5: 19.5: 20.5) in)

47 (48: 49: 50: 51) cm
(18.5 (19: 19.5: 19.5: 20) in)

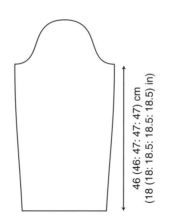

46 (46: 47: 47: 47) cm
(18 (18: 18.5: 18.5: 18.5) in)

No 13

# Ava

KIM HARGREAVES

## YARN

|  | XS | S | M | L | XL |
|---|---|---|---|---|---|
| To fit bust | 81 | 86 | 91 | 97 | 102 cm |
|  | 32 | 34 | 36 | 38 | 40 in |

**Rowan Ribbon Twist**

|  | 4 | 4 | 5 | 6 | 7 x 100gm |

(photographed in Rabble 118)

## NEEDLES

1 pair 12mm (US 17) needles

## TENSION

8 sts and 11 rows to 10 cm measured over reverse stocking stitch using 12mm (US 17) needles.

## BACK (worked from neck downwards)

Cast on 22 (22: 22: 24: 24) sts using 12mm (US 17) needles.
Beg with a P row, work in rev st st for 9 rows, ending with a RS row.
**Shape shoulders**
Cast on 2 sts at beg of next 2 rows.
26 (26: 26: 28: 28) sts.
Inc 1 st at each end of next 4 rows, then on foll 2 (3: 4: 4: 5) alt rows, then on every foll 4th row until there are 44 (46: 48: 50: 52) sts.
Cont straight until back measures 41 (42: 43: 44: 45) cm from cast-on edge, ending with a WS row.
**Shape lower edge**
Cast off 2 sts at beg of next row, then dec 1 st at end of foll row.
Rep last 2 rows once more. 38 (40: 42: 44: 46) sts.
Cast off 2 sts at beg of next row, then dec 1 st at each end of foll row. 34 (36: 38: 40: 42) sts.
Cast off 2 sts at beg and dec 1 st at end of next row, then dec 1 st at each end of foll row.
29 (31: 33: 35: 37) sts.

Rep last 2 rows 5 (5: 5: 6: 6) times more.
4 (6: 8: 5: 7) sts.
**S, M, L and XL sizes**
Cast off 2 sts at beg and dec 1 st at end of next row.
- (3: 5: 2: 4) sts.
**XS, M and XL sizes**
Dec 1 st at each end of next row. 2 (-: 3: -: 2) sts.
**All sizes**
**Next row:** (Work 2 tog) 1 (0: 0: 1: 1) times, (work 3 tog) 0 (1: 1: 0: 0) times and fasten off.

## FRONT

Work as given for back but working in st st, beg with a K row, to reverse RS of work.

## MAKING UP

**PRESS** as described on the information page.
Join both neck, shoulder and side seams using back stitch, or mattress stitch if preferred.

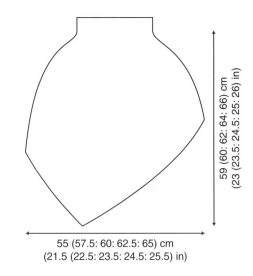

59 (60: 62: 64: 66) cm
(23 (23.5: 24.5: 25: 26) in)

55 (57.5: 60: 62.5: 65) cm
(21.5 (22.5: 23.5: 24.5: 25.5) in)

## No 14

# JILLY

### KIM HARGREAVES

**YARN**

|  | XS | S | M | L | XL |  |
|---|---|---|---|---|---|---|
| To fit bust | 81 | 86 | 91 | 97 | 102 | cm |
|  | 32 | 34 | 36 | 38 | 40 | in |

**Rowan Ribbon Twist**

|  | 7 | 7 | 7 | 8 | 8 | x 100gm |

(photographed in Racy 117)

**NEEDLES**

1 pair 10mm (no 000) (US 15) needles
1 pair 12mm (US 17) needles

**BUTTONS** – 1x00355

**TENSION**

8 sts and 11 rows to 10 cm measured over stocking stitch using 12mm (US 17) needles.

**Pattern note**: As row end edges form actual finished front opening edges of garment, it is important these edges are kept neat. Therefore avoid joining in new balls of yarn at these edges.

BACK AND FRONTS (worked in one piece to armholes)
Cast on 75 (81: 87: 87: 93) sts using 12mm (US 17) needles.
Work in border patt as folls:
**Rows 1 and 2:** Knit.
**Row 3 (RS):** K1, (K1, yfwd, K1) into next st, ★(K1 wrapping yarn twice round needle) 5 times, (K1, yfwd, K1, yfwd, K1) into next st, rep from ★ to last 7 sts, (K1 wrapping yarn twice round needle) 5 times, (K1, yfwd, K1) into next st, K1.
**Row 4:** K4, slip next 5 sts dropping extra loops, slip these 5 sts back onto left needle and P5tog, ★K5, slip next 5 sts dropping extra loops, slip these 5 sts back onto left needle and P5tog, rep from ★ to last 4 sts, K4.

**Rows 5 and 6:** Knit.
**Row 7:** K1, (K1 wrapping yarn twice round needle) 3 times, ★(K1, yfwd, K1, yfwd, K1) into next st, (K1 wrapping yarn twice round needle) 5 times, rep from ★ to last 5 sts, (K1, yfwd, K1, yfwd, K1) into next st, (K1 wrapping yarn twice round needle) 3 times, K1.
**Row 8:** K1, slip next 3 sts dropping extra loops, slip these 3 sts back onto left needle and P3tog, ★K5, slip next 5 sts dropping extra loops, slip these 5 sts back onto left needle and P5tog, rep from ★ to last 9 sts, K5, slip next 3 sts dropping extra loops, slip these 3 sts back onto left needle and P3tog, K1.
**Rows 9 to 12:** As rows 1 to 4.
These 12 rows complete border patt.
**XS and L sizes**
**Row 13:** K18 (-: -: 21: -), inc in next st, K37 (-: -: 43: -), inc in next st, K to end. 77 (-: -: 89: -) sts.
**S and XL sizes**
**Row 13:** Knit.
**M size**
**Row 13:** K21, K2tog, K41, K2tog, K to end. 85 sts.
**All sizes**
**Row 14 (WS):** K2, P to last 2 sts, K2.
**Row 15:** Knit.
Last 2 rows set the sts – front opening edge 2 sts (at both ends of rows) in garter st with all other sts in st st. Cont as set until work measures 29 (30: 30: 31: 31) cm, ending with a RS row.
**Divide for armholes**
**Next row (WS):** K2, P16 (17: 18: 19: 20) and slip these 18 (19: 20: 21: 22) sts onto a holder for left front, cast off 4 sts, P until there are 33 (35: 37: 39: 41) sts on right needle and turn, leaving rem 22 (23: 24: 25: 26) sts on another holder for right front.
**Shape back**
Work on this centre set of 33 (35: 37: 39: 41) sts only for back as folls:

Dec 1 st at each end of next 3 (3: 4: 4: 5) rows.
27 (29: 29: 31: 31) sts.
Cont straight until armhole measures 20 (20: 21: 21:
22) cm, ending with a WS row.

**Shape shoulders and back neck**

**Next row (RS):** Cast off 4 sts, K until there are
6 (7: 7: 7: 7) sts on right needle and turn, leaving
rem sts on a holder.
Work each side of neck separately.
Cast off 2 sts at beg of next row.
Cast off rem 4 (5: 5: 5: 5) sts.
With RS facing, rejoin yarn to rem sts, cast off
centre 7 (7: 7: 9: 9) sts, K to end.
Complete to match first side, reversing shapings.

**Shape left front**

With RS facing, rejoin yarn to 18 (19: 20: 21: 22) sts
left on holder for left front and cont as folls:
Dec 1 st at armhole edge of next 3 (3: 4: 4: 5) rows.
15 (16: 16: 17: 17) sts.
Cont straight until 7 (7: 7: 9: 9) rows less have been
worked than on back to start of shoulder shaping,
ending with a RS row.

**Shape neck**

Cast off 4 sts at beg of next row.
11 (12: 12: 13: 13) sts.
Dec 1 st at neck edge of next 2 rows, then on foll
1 (1: 1: 2: 2) alt rows. 8 (9: 9: 9: 9) sts.
Work 2 rows, ending with a WS row.

**Shape shoulder**

Cast off 4 sts at beg of next row.
Work 1 row. Cast off rem 4 (5: 5: 5: 5) sts.

**Shape right front**

With **WS** facing, rejoin yarn to 22 (23: 24: 25: 26) sts
left on holder for right front, cast off 4 sts, P to last
2 sts, K2. 18 (19: 20: 21: 22) sts.
Dec 1 st at armhole edge of next 3 (3: 4: 4: 5) rows.
15 (16: 16: 17: 17) sts.
Cont straight until 3 rows less have been worked
than on left front to start of neck shaping, ending
with a WS row.

**Next row (buttonhole row) (RS):** K3, yfwd,
K2tog, K to end.
Work 3 rows, ending with a WS row.

**Shape neck**

Cast off 4 sts at beg of next row. 11 (12: 12: 13: 13) sts.
Dec 1 st at neck edge of next 2 rows, then on foll 1
(1: 1: 2: 2) alt rows. 8 (9: 9: 9: 9) sts.

Work 2 rows, ending with a RS row.

**Shape shoulder**

Cast off 4 sts at beg of next row.
Work 1 row. Cast off rem 4 (5: 5: 5: 5) sts.

SLEEVES (both alike)
Cast on 27 sts using 12mm (US 17) needles.
Work in border patt as given for back and fronts for
8 rows.
Beg with a K row, cont in st st as folls:

**M, L and XL sizes**

Inc 1 st at each end of – (–: 17th: 17th: 13th) and
foll – (–: 0: 0: 12th) row. – (–: 29: 29: 31) sts.

**All sizes**

Cont straight until sleeve measures 43 (43: 44: 44:
44) cm, ending with a WS row.

**Shape top**

Cast off 2 sts at beg of next 2 rows.
23 (23: 25: 25: 27) sts.
Dec 1 st at each end of next and foll alt row, then
on every foll 4th row to 15 (15: 17: 17: 19) sts, then
on 1 (1: 2: 2: 3) foll alt rows, then on foll row,
ending with a WS row. Cast off rem 11 sts.

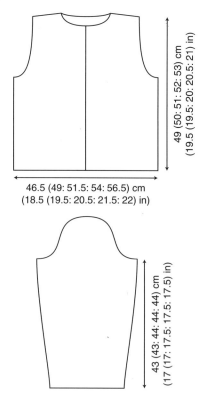

46.5 (49: 51.5: 54: 56.5) cm
(18.5 (19.5: 20.5: 21.5: 22) in)

49 (50: 51: 52: 53) cm
(19.5 (19.5: 20: 20.5: 21) in)

43 (43: 44: 44: 44) cm
(17 (17: 17.5: 17.5: 17.5) in)

## MAKING UP
**PRESS** as described on the information page. Join both shoulder seams using back stitch, or mattress stitch if preferred.

**Neckband**

With RS facing and using 10mm (US 15) needles, starting and ending at front opening edges, pick up and knit 13 (13: 13: 15: 15) sts up right side of neck, 12 (12: 12: 14: 14) sts from back, then 13 (13: 13: 15: 15) sts down left side of neck.
38 (38: 38: 44: 44) sts.
Cast off knitwise (on WS).
See information page for finishing instructions, setting in sleeves using the set-in method.

# No 15

# MERCY

KIM HARGREAVES

## YARN
One size
**Rowan Ribbon Twist**
   2      x      100gm
(photographed in Rocky 113)

## NEEDLES
1 pair 8mm (no 0) (US 11) needles
1 pair 12mm (US 17) needles

## TENSION
8 sts and 11 rows to 10 cm measured over stocking stitch using 12mm (US 17) needles.

**Pattern note:** Unless stated otherwise, all slipped sts should be slipped purlwise.

## BERET
Cast on 45 sts using 8mm (US 11) needles.
Work in garter st for 3 rows, ending with a **WS** row.
Change to 12mm (US 17) needles.
**Row 1 (RS):** K1, (sl 1, K3) 11 times.
**Row 2:** (K3, P1) 11 times, K1.
**Row 3:** K1, (sl 1, K2, M1, K1) 11 times. 56 sts.
**Row 4:** (K4, P1) 11 times, K1.

**Row 5:** K1, (sl 1, K4) 11 times.
**Row 6:** As row 4.
**Row 7:** K1, (sl 1, K3, M1, K1) 11 times. 67 sts.
**Row 8:** (K5, P1) 11 times, K1.
**Row 9:** K1, (sl 1, K5) 11 times.
**Rows 10 to 17:** As rows 8 and 9, 4 times.
**Row 18:** As row 8.
**Row 19:** K1, (sl 1, K3, K2tog tbl) 11 times. 56 sts.
**Rows 20 to 22:** As rows 4 to 6.
**Row 23:** K1, (sl 1, K2, K2tog tbl) 11 times. 45 sts.
**Row 24:** As row 2.
**Rows 25 and 26:** As rows 1 and 2.
**Row 27:** K1, (sl 1, K1, K2tog tbl) 11 times. 34 sts.
**Row 28:** (K2, P1) 11 times, K1.
**Row 29:** K1, (sl 1, K2tog tbl) 11 times. 23 sts.
**Row 30:** (K1, P1) 11 times, K1.
**Row 31:** K1, (sl 1 **knitwise**, K1, psso) 11 times.
Break yarn and thread through rem 12 sts. Pull up tight and fasten off securely.

## MAKING UP
**PRESS** as described on the information page.
Join back seam. Make a 7 cm diameter pompom and attach to top of beret.

# INFORMATION PAGE

### TENSION

Obtaining the correct tension is perhaps the single factor which can make the difference between a successful garment and a disastrous one. It controls both the shape and size of an article, so **any** variation, can distort the finished look of the garment. We recommend that you knit a square in pattern and/or stocking stitch of perhaps 5 more stitches and rows than those given in the tension note. Press the finished square under a damp cloth and mark out the central 10cm square. If you have too many stitches to 10cm try again using thicker needles, if you have too few stitches to 10cm try again using finer needles.

### SIZING AND SIZE DIAGRAM NOTE

The instructions are given for the smallest size. Where they vary, work the figures in brackets for the larger sizes. **One set of figures refers to all sizes**. Included with every pattern in this magazine is a '**size diagram**', the purpose of which is to enable you to accurately achieve a perfect fitting garment without the need for worry during knitting. The size diagram shows the finished width of the garment at the under-arm point, and it is this measurement that the knitter should choose first. Next look at the corresponding length for that size; if you are not happy with the total length which we recommend, adjust your own garment before beginning your armhole shaping - any adjustment after this point will mean that your sleeve will not fit into your garment easily - don't forget to take your adjustment into account if there is any side seam shaping. Finally, look at the sleeve length; the size diagram shows the finished sleeve measurement, taking into account any top-arm insertion length. Measure your body between the centre of your neck and your wrist, this measurement should correspond to half the garment width plus the sleeve length. Again, your sleeve length may be adjusted, but remember to take into consideration your sleeve increases if you do adjust the length - you must increase more frequently than the pattern states to shorten your sleeve, less frequently to lengthen it.

### FINISHING INSTRUCTIONS

After working for hours knitting a garment, it seems a great pity that many garments are spoiled because such little care is taken in the pressing and finishing process.

### PRESSING

Darn in all ends neatly along the selvage edge or a colour join, as appropriate. Block out each piece of knitting using pins and gently press each piece, omitting the ribs, using a warm iron over a damp cloth. **Tip**: Take special care to press the edges, as this will make sewing up both easier and neater.

### STITCHING

When stitching the pieces together, remember to match areas of colour and texture very carefully where they meet.
Use a seam stitch such as back stitch or mattress stitch for all main knitting seams, and join all ribs and neckband with a flat seam unless otherwise stated.

### CONSTRUCTION

Having completed the pattern instructions, join left shoulder and neckband seams as detailed above.
Sew the top of the sleeve to the body of the garment using the method detailed in the pattern, referring to the appropriate guide:
**Square set-in sleeves:** Set sleeve head into armhole, the straight sides at top of sleeve to form a neat right-angle to cast-off sts at armhole on back and front.
**Shallow set-in sleeves:** Join cast-off sts at beg of armhole shaping to cast-off sts at start of sleeve-head

shaping. Sew sleeve head into armhole, easing in shapings.
**Set-in sleeves:** Set in sleeve, easing sleeve head into armhole.

Join side and sleeve seams.
Slip stitch pocket edgings and linings into place.
Sew on buttons to correspond with buttonholes.
After sewing up, press seams and hems.
Ribbed welts and neckbands and any areas of garter stitch should not be pressed.

## EXPERIENCE RATINGS

●      =    Easy, straight forward knitting

● ●    =    Suitable for the average knitter

## ABBREVIATIONS

| | |
|---|---|
| **K** | knit |
| **P** | purl |
| **st(s)** | stitch(es) |
| **inc** | increas(e)(ing) |
| **dec** | decreas(e)(ing) |
| **st st** | stocking stitch (1 row K, 1 row P) |
| **garter st** | garter stitch (K every row) |
| **beg** | begin(ning) |
| **foll** | following |
| **rem** | remain(ing) |
| **rev** | revers(e)(ing) |
| **rep** | repeat |
| **alt** | alternate |
| **cont** | continue |
| **patt** | pattern |
| **tog** | together |
| **mm** | millimetres |
| **cm** | centimetres |
| **in(s)** | inch(es) |
| **RS** | right side |
| **WS** | wrong side |
| **sl1** | slip one stitch |
| **p2sso** | pass 2 slipped stitches over |
| **tbl** | through back of loop |
| **M1** | make one stitch by picking up horizontal loop before next stitch and knitting into back of it |
| **M1P** | make one stitch by picking up horizontal loop before next stitch and purling into back of it |
| **yfwd** | yarn forward |
| **cn** | cable needle |

# STOCKIST INFORMATION
## ROWAN OVERSEAS DISTRIBUTORS

**AUSTRALIA**
Australian Country Spinners
314 Albert Street,
Brunswick
Victoria 3056.
Tel: (03) 9380 3888

**BELGIUM**
Pavan
Meerlaanstraat 73
B9860 Balegem (Oosterzele)
Tel: (32) 9 221 8594

**CANADA**
Diamond Yarn
9697 St Laurent,
Montreal
Quebec H3L 2N1
Tel: (514) 388 6188
www.diamondyarns.com

Diamond Yarn ( Toronto )
155 Martin Ross,
Unit 3
Toronto,
Ontario M3J 2L9
Tel: (416) 736 6111
www.diamondyarns.com

**DENMARK**
Individual stockists –
please contact Rowan for details

**FRANCE**
Elle Tricote
8 Rue du Coq
67000 Strasbourg
Tel: (33) 3 88 23 03 13
www.elletricote.com

**GERMANY**
Wolle & Design
Wolfshovener Strasse 76
52428 Julich-Stetternich
Tel : (49) 2461 54735.
www.wolleundesign.de

**HOLLAND**
de Afstap
Oude Leliestraat 12
1015 AW Amsterdam
Tel : (31) 20 6231445

**HONG KONG**
East Unity Co Ltd
Unit B2
7/F, Block B
Kailey Industrial Centre
12 Fung Yip Street
Chai Wan
Tel : (852) 2869 7110.

**ICELAND**
Storkurinn
Laugavegi 59
Reykjavik
Tel: (354) 551 82 58

**JAPAN**
Puppy Co Ltd
TOC Building
7-22-17 Nishigotanda
Shinagwa-Ku
Tokyo
Tel : (81) 3 3494 2435

**NEW ZEALAND**
Individual stockists –
please contact Rowan for details

**NORWAY**
Pa Pinne
Tennisun 3D
0777 OSLO
Tel: (47) 909 62 818
www.paapinne.no

**SWEDEN**
Wincent
Norrtulsgaten 65
11345 Stockholm
Tel: (46) 8 673 70 60

**U.S.A**.
Rowan USA
4 Townsend West
Suite 8,
Nashua
New Hampshire 03063
Tel: (1 603) 886 5041/5043

For details of U.K. stockists or any other information
concerning this book please contact:

Rowan Yarns, Green Lane Mill, Holmfirth,
West Yorkshire HD9 2DX
Tel: +44 (0)1484 681881   Fax: +44 (0)1484 687920
Email: ribbontwist@knitrowan.com www.knitrowan.com

Photographer Joey Toller • Styling Kim Hargreaves • Hair & Make-up Annabel Hobbs • Model Marina Shekel
Thank you to John Bischoff for the use of his studio. Tel: 020 7278 8006 Email: Johnbischoff@lineone.net

Mercy